BROKEN
MOTHER, BROKEN CHILD

HEALING THE WOUNDS FROM ATTACHMENT TRAUMA

DR. SHARON BATY

Womenspeak Recovery Publishing

Copyright ©2024 by

ALL RIGHTS RESERVED

No part of this publication may be reproduced, stored in a retrieval system, or transmitted in any form or by any means, e.g., electronic, mechanical, photocopy, recording, or otherwise, without the express prior permission of the author, except for brief excerpts in magazine articles, reviews, and personal or small group study.

Requests for translating into other languages should be addressed to the author.

This book is dedicated to all the men and women who have embarked on their journey of healing from the effects of attachment trauma

CONTENTS

Introduction	vii
1. Mother and Child Attachment	1
2. What Is a Mother?	3
3. Women's Ethnic and Cultural Perspectives of Motherhood	17
4. Male Perspectives on Motherhood:	23
5. Men's Ethnic and Cultural	31
6. Learning Motherhood by Proxy-Breaking Unintentionally	35
7. Attachment Trauma:	41
8. Types of Mothers	51
9. The Adult Child:	61
10. Healing the Wounded Child Within	67
11. The Good Imperfect Mother	69
Bibliography	73

INTRODUCTION

When we think about a mother, certain timeless qualities may come to mind. We imagine a figure who is nurturing, enveloping her children in a warm embrace of love and protection. A mother is often seen as forgiving and gentle, a steady presence providing unwavering support and understanding. These characteristics form the ideal image of motherhood, a cornerstone of our emotional foundation.

A little girl often learns how to nurture and love by observing and receiving care from her mother. This relationship teaches her the subtleties of empathy, kindness, and affection, shaping her future interactions and her approach to life. Similarly, boys frequently derive their understanding of sensitivity, respect, and how to treat women from the way that their mothers treat them. This maternal influence is profound, serving as a blueprint for their future relationships and emotional responses.

But what if this ideal is shattered? What if the mother is not nurturing, not gentle, not protective, or not encouraging? What if she is cold, dismissive, disconnected, or even overtly abusive? How does this deviation from the ideal maternal norm affect a child's development? How does it shape the child's emotional and psychological landscape in adolescence and adulthood?

Consider the daughter subjected to a mother's emotional coldness and neglect. Will she inevitably mirror the behavior she witnessed, becoming a reflection of her mother's deficiencies? Will she struggle to break free from the cycle of disconnection and emotional pain? What of the son raised without the warmth and support of a loving mother? Will he find it challenging to trust, love, and respect women due to being haunted by the absence of maternal affection during his formative years?

In this book, we embark on a journey to explore the deep and lasting impact of emotionally abusive mothers. This book delves into various perspectives and personal narratives to uncover the intricate ways in which dysfunctional maternal behavior influences a child's growth. We will examine the specific effects on both daughters and sons, exploring how a mother's neglect, criticism, physical abuse, mental illness, and physical absence manifest in the lives of her daughters and sons.

Understanding the traumas that shape these mothers' behaviors is crucial. We will investigate mothers' behavioral histories, uncovering cycles of abuse, abandonment, and mental illness that perpetuate these damaging patterns. By shedding light on these root causes, we aim to break the cycle of abuse and pave the way for healing.

Healing is not only possible but also essential for the wounded adult child of an emotionally abusive mother. This journey involves acknowledging the pain, embracing reparenting techniques, and seeking therapy and support systems. Through these steps, individuals can reclaim their sense of self-worth and build healthier relationships, thereby breaking free from the chains of their past.

Broken Mother, Broken Child: Healing the Wounds from Attachment Trauma is more than a study of dysfunction and pain; it is a testament to the resilience of the human spirit and the possibility of positive transformation. It is a call to understand, heal, and foster environments in which the true essence of motherhood—one of nurturing, warmth, and unconditional love—can flourish. Through this exploration, we hope to inspire a deeper understanding of the profound impact that mothers have on their children and the importance of breaking the cycle of the mother's emotional abuse and neglect.

Reflection Questions

1. How important was your mother in your life when you were growing up?
2. What do you think that the term "broken mother" means?

CHAPTER 1
MOTHER AND CHILD ATTACHMENT

One of the most important relationships that a child experiences is the relationship with the mother. The mother carries the child for nine months, so the mother–child bond starts long before the child takes his or her first breath. The mother is often the first person the newborn child lays his or her eyes on after birth; many newborns go from their mother's womb straight into her arms.

The bond between mother and child is often strengthened as the child grows older, from the pivotal early stages of physical and psychosocial development. However, for some mothers and children, this important bond gets weakened over time, while for some other children, this bond never develops properly.

One of the most widely recognized theories of attachment was developed by John Bowlby. He suggested that to create a healthy secure attachment in the child, the mother must consistently provide for the child's basic needs (including nourishment, comfort, and safety). He also believed that the mother's role is to nurture the child's character, creating a foundation from which the child can navigate the world socially. The mother helps to develop the child's overall sense of self-worth and psychological wellbeing. The attachment formed between the mother and child often creates a blueprint for the way in which he or she relates to other people.

It is important to recognize that the attachment and bonding between mother and child is not always the beautiful and magical process that is seen in many movies or that is described by other mothers. There are many factors that may interfere with what is supposed to be a natural bonding experience between mother and child. Furthermore, whether there is a strong bond between mother and child at birth, the role that she plays in the child's life throughout childhood may prove to be just as important, perhaps even more important.

Reflection Questions

1. Do you think that children who did not develop a close bond with their mother will have difficultly as they age in close relationships with friends and romantic partners? Why or why not?
2. How would you describe your attachment to your mother?
3. How do you think that attachment has influenced the way you express yourself physically and emotionally?
4. What would have strengthened your attachment to your mother?

CHAPTER 2
WHAT IS A MOTHER?
PERSPECTIVES ON MOTHERHOOD: ROLE OF MOTHERS FOR DAUGHTERS

Women all over the world view motherhood through various perspectives. Each offers unique insights into what it means to be a mother. These perspectives are influenced by many factors, including societal expectations, personal aspirations, and the delicate balance between professional duties and family life. Motherhood is a multifaceted experience, rich with a diversity of perspectives shaped by individual backgrounds, cultural contexts, and personal journeys.

How Women View Motherhood

For some women, motherhood is the ultimate expression of love and selflessness. It may be a role that they have anticipated eagerly and embraced gladly. They may find deep fulfillment in nurturing their children and watching them grow. These mothers often describe the experience as transformative, teaching them patience, resilience, and a profound sense of purpose. The bond that they share with their children becomes a cornerstone of their identity, shaping their daily lives and future aspirations.

Other women approach motherhood with a blend of excitement and apprehension, recognizing both the joys and the immense responsibilities that motherhood entails. They navigate the challenges of balancing career ambitions with the demands of raising a family, juggling the pressure to excel in both arenas. For these mothers, finding harmony between their personal and professional lives is an ongoing challenge that requires constant adjustments and self-reflection.

There are also women for whom the decision to become a mother is fraught with ambivalence or outright reluctance. They may grapple with societal expectations that equate womanhood with motherhood. They may feel conflicted about having children. For these women, the journey to motherhood, if it happens, can be accompanied by a mix of emotions, including guilt, fear, anxiety, ambivalence, and uncertainty. However, despite such misgivings, if they do choose to embrace motherhood, they may find their own unique ways to integrate it into their lives, redefining what it means to be a mother on their own terms.

Cultural background plays a significant role in shaping women's views on motherhood. In some cultures, motherhood is revered and considered a vital part of a woman's identity, with strong community support systems in place for mothers. In other societies, women might experience more freedom to define their roles independently, leading to a broader spectrum of what is acceptable for motherhood to look like. This cultural diversity highlights the importance of acknowledging and respecting different perspectives and experiences.

Ultimately, the female perspective on motherhood is as diverse as women themselves. Each woman's story can add a valuable dimension to our understanding of what it means to be a mother. By listening to and honoring these varied experiences, we can gain a richer and more inclusive view of motherhood that celebrates both the shared elements and the unique journeys of women everywhere.

The definition of a mother varies, depending on who is being asked. There are definitions specific to culture. From a Christian biblical perspective, Proverbs 31:27 states that a mother takes care of her household, stays busy, and does not give in to the temptation of laziness. She stays productive and gets to work early. She takes her time completing her responsibilities. However, some people would say that a mother is more than the sum of her duties. Instead, she is an integral part of the healthy growth and development of a child. She is the emotional and physical anchor, providing the foundation for her children and the entire family.

The role of the mother for her daughter is highly subjective and is specific to each culture, among many other variables. Some consider traditional gender roles to be normative. Others do not. However, the desire for mothers to be nurturing is a near-universal expectation, even if not always expressed explicitly.

A mother's role and responsibilities to her daughter include teaching the following:

- mentoring (leading by example)
- carrying herself
- navigating the world as a female
- caring for herself (hygiene and grooming)
- nurturing others
- relating to romantic partners
- imparting lessons that she has learned so her daughter does not repeat the same mistakes
- setting boundaries with romantic partners

- defining the meaning of unconditional love

Katie, a 19-year-old Anglo woman, would agree that her mother, despite her own challenges with relationships and other traumas, fulfilled most of these roles and responsibilities. For some mothers, these roles and responsibilities are overwhelming.

Katie was the oldest of three siblings. She took on the role of surrogate mother because her mother was the sole provider for Katie and her siblings. She was responsible for her siblings almost all the time when her mom was working. Despite Katie's mother's being a single parent for most of her life, Katie's mother showed up in a way that made a significant impact on Katie's definition of what a mother's role is. Katie's mother was a counselor, protector, nurturer, and provider.

Katie stated,

"If I ever called her saying [that] I was having a mental crisis, she would be on her way to listen and care for me without judgment. My mother's role [when I was] growing up was to nurture, care, and provide for us. When I was growing up, my biological father was abusive, so this caused my mother to protect me."

Katie further described her relationship with her mother as "very good" and "very stable," especially when Katie was younger. She stated, however, that when she became a teenager, she became rebellious. She stated, "I only cared about boys, drugs, and sex. And that put our relationship at a standstill."

At age 19, Katie was able to acknowledge her mother's constructive parenting efforts and her own normal but problematic adolescent acting out. Katie became a mother herself a few months ago.

Perhaps the life-transforming experience of becoming a mother influenced Katie's level of insight into the challenges of motherhood. She stated,

> "One of the strong memories I have with my mother was the day I had my daughter. I wanted to give up because my body was tired and distressed from all the pain and the pushing [that] I was doing. Watching and hearing my mom tell me that I could do it and not to give up and hearing, 'One more push and you'll have your daughter in your arms' has stuck with me."

The mother–daughter relationship may have stages or may evolve over time, as in Katie's case. Some would say that Katie is lucky to have a mother who had such a strong influence on her, a mother who provided an example for how Katie could mother her own child.

Evolving relationships between mother and daughter are as unique as the daughter and mother themselves. In Taya's experience, her witness of emotional and verbal abuse by her father towards her mother made Taya despise her mother. In a gender and sex psychology class, Taya was asked to write about what it means to be a woman and the role her mother played in shaping her identity. She wrote:

> "Where do we learn about what it means to be a male or female? For me, it was clear: To be female, I was supposed to be just like my mother. I was supposed to keep my physical appearance up, learn how to cook a great meal, take care of the kids, and be a submissive good wife. I was to get married to a man who would take care of me, and in return, I would

give him all of me: my mind and my body. [I would] learn to deny my own wishes, desires, and opinions.

"I was to understand that my man would be a man. [This] was code language for 'men will stray' or cheat because it was in their nature, but being a good wife meant [that] I would swallow my pride and my own feelings of betrayal and just accept my role as the dedicated wife, superwoman, and mother to my husband's children.

"I learned all of this by watching my mother. The power my father had over my mother made her a victim [who was] full of fear [and] unable to speak or move. [This made] her powerless and eventually resulted in the death of her spirit. I remember watching the deterioration of my mother for a few years. At the young age of 12, I remember thinking, 'That will never be me.'"

Taya struggled with anger towards her mother, not only because Taya felt that her mom was too weak to stand up to Taya's father but also because Taya indicated that her mother did not prepare Taya to navigate the world as a woman. She stated that she sought other female examples. She wanted to find women whom she respected as role models.

When she became the mother of a daughter, Taya decided that she would do the opposite of what her mother did when it came to self-advocacy and respect. Taya vowed to teach her daughter not to allow any man to disrespect her for any reason. The choice Taya made was representative of counter-imitation: Taya mothered in a way opposite to the way in which she had been mothered. She was deliberate and conscious about what she would teach her daughter. When asked, she stated, "For my daughter, I was a teacher, a counselor, a doctor, a disciplinarian, a coach, a cheerleader, and a provider of emotional and financial support. I taught her never to depend on a man for support."

Some might say that Taya's approach to mothering was extreme and fueled by anger. Others would say that her own pain and bitterness made her redefine motherhood. Eventually, Taya disclosed that after her own healing from not being mothered the way she felt that she needed to be mothered, she found understanding and compassion when she realized that her mother had given her what she knew. What her mother knew was to stay with the father of her children and maintain a two-parent home, no matter what. That was what her mother deemed as good responsible mothering.

Taya stated that she recognized that although her mother did not have the knowledge or tools to give Taya effective ways in which to navigate the world, what her mother did give her—which was important—was how to love unconditionally, even when this was hard. It was then that she could add what she was teaching her daughter, which was not only the importance of loving unconditionally but also how to forgive. As Taya put it,

> "Eventually, I had to forgive my mom for not giving me what I felt that I needed. It was easier to forgive her when I realized that she did give me something: She taught me how to be a mother through the way she mothered me. Here's the kicker: She mothered me the opposite way from how she was mothered because she was adopted and experienced abuse and neglect. I am forever grateful that I asked questions to my mom about what she'd been through."

A mother gives her daughter what she has; she can only give to her kids what she has been given or what she has learned. This teaches us compassion and understanding without the desire to minimize or deny the needs we had as a child that were not met.

Taya stated that she struggled with trusting in relationships with men due to seeing the interactions between her mom and her dad. Taya stated that she felt that her mother failed to protect Taya from being exposed to the abuse between her parents.

Many may believe that the daughter's first experience of an intimate relationship serves as an important foundation on which she builds future relationships with romantic partners and children. Others state that the mother's connection with the daughter has a significant impact on her self-esteem as she gets older. Suzanne Degges-White agrees. She's the author of *Mothers and Daughters: Living, Loving, and Learning Over a Lifetime*. Ethnic culture is a significant factor in how children view the roles and responsibilities of the mother.

Jade, a 22-year-old African-American girl, was asked, "What is the role of a mother?" She replied,

> "A mother is the nurturer, and she is the one the kids go to for comfort, especially when they are hurt. They always call for their mom, and she kisses the wounds, and the kid feels better. But as the kid gets older, moms teach their kids to be strong and not to let anyone push them around."

Jade may be implying that the mom is the child's main source of physical and psychological support. The mom helps her children to process their emotions, especially the hard ones. However, independent problem-solving is expected as kids age.

Sally, a 51-year-old biracial woman (African-American and Native-American), was 10 years old when her mother died. Sally indicated that she remembered being close to her mom, although she struggled with depression. Sally stated, "She slept a lot and often asked me to lie next to her and stroke her hair." Not realizing that her mom struggled with chronic depression and was never treated for it, Sally stated that her mom would shut down (disengage from her, her siblings and father), and isolate, refusing to talk:

> "My mom taught school for many years but did a dance move for a show she was rehearsing and injured her ligaments and was disabled. She became a stay-at-home mom, and while she loved it, I suspect she lost her identity and ability to see her purpose. I was close to my mom. She was present for school events, taught a gifted program at our elementary school, and created the cheerleader team. At home, she was either cooking, talking on the phone, or sleeping."

Sally stated that she saw that her mother's role was to educate, provide for, and nurture her and her sibling. Despite her mom's mental illness, Sally stated, "She was charismatic. She taught school, poetry, and plays. She would go to dinner parties."

Stephane, a 49-year-old Anglo woman, stated,

> "My mother's influence on the person I see staring back at me in the mirror is significant. It has not diminished over the years. She taught me values and principles about life, and those have influenced my choices as an adult, my relationships, and my ambitions. She always encouraged me to think for myself."

Stephane's experience was unusual in that her mother had her when she was in her late forties. Stephanie reported that because her mom was established in her career and was financially stable, she had more to invest in "hands-on, authoritative" parenting. Stephanie's mother never got married and became impregnated via a sperm donor. When asked if she wondered who her father was, Stephane stated, "Sometimes. But I don't feel like I missed out on anything."

Victoria, a 33-year-old Hispanic female, had a mom who was physically present but emotionally absent. Victoria spoke of understanding why this was the case. However, she still acknowledges her need for the emotional support that she never received from her mom. Victoria said,

> "My mom was always there. She was a nurturer and taught me and my sisters to be strong. But I felt sometimes when I wanted that closeness with her that she was distant. The times when I wanted her to hold me, she wouldn't do that. I saw that [distance] in her parents, too. I'm not saying my mom didn't know how to love because there are times when I would be crying, and she was there to comfort me. Maybe I wanted more."

Victoria's healing process continues as she works on her abandonment issues in therapy.

> "As I continue to age, I am starting to understand my mom. A lot of the trauma I have with my mom is generational. It's OK that my relationship with her is different than mine and my dad's.
>
> "We connect on a different level. It's healthy for the most part, but there are times when she nitpicks—for example, when she brings up my melasma (dark spots) on my face. I

guess I should be fortunate that it's not something having to do with my weight."

At times, Victoria struggles with feeling that she must endure her mom's continual emotional and verbal abuse, as if Victoria is required to be an emotional and verbal punching bag "in the name of loyalty." Victoria's focus is to try to maintain some type of connection but not at the expense of her self-esteem. The quandary that Victoria finds herself in isn't unique; there is a younger child-like part of her that wants her mom, whereas the adult rational part knows that her mother does not seem to be able to be gentle, loving, or supportive.

Preta, a 29-year-old Asian-American woman, has had an experience like Victoria's. Preta is also an adult whose child part desires a connection, but she talks herself out of the need for that connection, finding herself struggling with both dislike and codependency. Preta stated,

"I am not going to get what I want from this lady. I need her to be present and communicate what is going on in our lives. She has always been kinda neglectful. She would always drop me off when I was a child. We never did the mother–daughter bonding. She did not think it was necessary. She did her best holding down the house. She was distant. Now I live with her, and I feel like I must get her out of her shell. I would love for her to connect with me—like friends—instead of her talking down to me. I wish that we could share interests other than what we see on the news.

"She makes excuses about being too tired and needing to zone out. I did not have her as a mother as a little girl or now. It took a lot for her to raise me. She did a lot of the raising of me and my sister. I want to bond with my mom. My mom and her mom were distant. She was one of six girls. But what I've learned is that she cannot be responsible for my emotions as an adult. But it's still hard."

Preta indicated that she realizes that her mom's time now costs something. stating that if she helps her mom with meeting the goals she has, she can have quality time with her. She admitted that the behavior of paying people for getting emotional needs met has played out in adult friendships and romantic relationships.

Patterns of maternal functioning are passed down to the daughters through the mother's mothering and interactions with the daughter. The beautifully done 1993 film *The Joy Luck Club* (based on the 1989 novel by Amy Tan) depicts the complicated relationship between Chinese immigrant mothers and their American-born daughters.

In one of its many powerful scenes, Ying Ying St. Clair teaches her daughter about recognizing and acknowledging what she wants and deserves. The mother encourages her daughter to leave an emotionally abusive relationship. Ying Ying attempts to save her daughter from what appears to be dependency and fear:

Ying Ying (the mother) asks Lena (her daughter) "Do you know what you want from him?"

Lena replies, "Respect. Tenderness."

Ying Ying states, "Then tell him now, and leave this lopsided house, and don't come back until he gives you those things with both hands open."

Lena looks down tearfully and states, "I can't."

Ying Ying looks at her daughter as if channeling her own younger self and states, "Losing him does not matter; it is you that will be found and cherished."

What a scene of healing and vulnerability for Ying Ying and her daughter! This scene is a powerful example of emotional intimacy between mother and daughter. The mother, although she went through significant emotional trauma from being in an abusive relationship and guilt associated with the loss of her son, can make meaning from those traumas and help her daughter.

Mothers sometimes find that their best advice to their daughters comes from their own recovery from pain. The roles, responsibilities, and expectations of mothers from different ethnic cultures have similarities and differences.

Reflection Questions

1. What do you believe was the role of your mother?
2. Do you feel that your mother fulfilled the roles you expected or wanted her to fulfill? Explain.
3. If you are a mother, how well do you fulfill the role of mother? Explain.

CHAPTER 3

WOMEN'S ETHNIC AND CULTURAL PERSPECTIVES OF MOTHERHOOD

PERSPECTIVE OF FEMALE AFRICAN AMERICANS

For African-American women, motherhood holds great cultural significance, deeply rooted in a history of resilience, community, and strength. Historically, African-American mothers have been the backbone of their families, often bearing the weight of both nurturing their children and supporting their communities. This role is celebrated and respected, symbolizing a deep-seated commitment to family and cultural continuity.

African-American mothers frequently draw upon rich cultural traditions to instill values of pride, perseverance, and identity in their children. These traditions often include storytelling, music, and communal gatherings that reinforce a sense of belonging and cultural heritage. The importance of extended family and community support is also a hallmark of African-American motherhood. Grandmothers, aunts, and other relatives play integral roles in child-rearing.

However, African-American mothers face unique challenges that can add layers of complexity to their experiences. Systemic issues, such as racial discrimination, economic disparities, and limited access to quality healthcare and education, can be major stressors. Single parenthood can exacerbate other stressors, which may influence the way in which African-American women mother their children. These obstacles create a challenge: Sink or swim. Despite daunting challenges, many African-American mothers exhibit remarkable strength and resilience.

Balancing these difficulties while striving to provide the best for their children often means that African-American mothers must navigate a world that can be supportive and adversarial. Despite these challenges, their ability to foster strong, loving families and communities remains a testament to their enduring spirit.

Perspective of Female Hispanics

In Hispanic cultures, the role of the mother is often central to family life, deeply filled with cultural significance and expectations. The mother is typically seen as the heart of the household, responsible not only for nurturing and caregiving but also for maintaining family traditions and values. Her presence is a cornerstone of stability and emotional support. Many Hispanic mothers hold the additional role of primary provider of financial stability. They also play a significant role in ensuring their children get the education they need to be successful when they get older.

Perspective of Female Anglos

Anglo women's perspectives on parenthood are diverse and represent both ancient and modern beliefs. In the past, the Anglo perspective has frequently highlighted the value of family and the mother's position as the head of the home. But modern changes—

driven by shifting cultural standards and individual goals—have brought more complicated and nuanced approaches to parenthood.

Traditionally, Anglo women were often seen as the primary caregivers within the family. They were responsible for bringing up children and maintaining the home. This view was deeply rooted in cultural and religious beliefs, in which motherhood was considered a woman's most important and fulfilling role. The traditional Anglo mother was expected to be nurturing, self-sacrificing, and dedicated to the wellbeing of her family.

Modern views on motherhood among Anglo women have evolved. Today, many Anglo women seek to balance their roles as mothers with their professional ambitions and their personal interests. The modern perspective embraces more flexibility and diversity about what it means to be a mother. Women can thrive in multiple roles simultaneously, even though doing so poses challenges, such as time management. This shift has been driven by women's increased access to education and career opportunities, changing gender norms, and a growing recognition of the importance of shared parenting responsibilities.

Many modern Anglo mothers strive for a more equitable distribution of household duties and childcare with their partners. They value independence and the ability to pursue their own goals while being deeply committed to their children. This approach has led to a dynamic and multi-faceted view of motherhood that respects individual choice and diverse experiences.

Perspective of Female Native Americans

Native-American women offer a unique perspective on motherhood, deeply rooted in their cultural heritage and traditions. For many Indigenous communities, motherhood is revered as a sacred and essential role within the family and the broader community. However, the impact of maternal absence on child development is a complex and often overlooked aspect of this perspective.

In many Native-American cultures, the maternal figure serves as the primary caregiver and nurturer, imparting essential teachings, traditions, and values to the next generation. The absence of a mother due to various factors such as historical trauma, systemic injustices, or contemporary challenges including substance abuse or incarceration can have a great effect on a child's development.

Perspective of Female Asian Americans

The mother's position is extremely important in many Asian cultures, influencing not only the dynamics within the family but also the identities of the individual and the expectations of society. On the other hand, the experience of having a mother absent can have a significant impact on the views that Asian-American women have about parenthood and their identity.

In traditional Asian communities, the mother is frequently seen as the primary nurturer and caretaker, the adult in charge of establishing the family's welfare, imparting morals, and offering emotional support. For her children, she provides stability and direction by being a constant and reliable presence in their lives.

Asian-American women may strive to embody the nurturing qualities they associate with their own mothers. They may draw inspiration from their memories while forging their own path as mothers. This may come through conscious efforts to be present or by reimagining traditional notions of caregiving.

At the same time, the influence of cultural expectations on Asian Americans cannot be overlooked. Asian societies often place a high premium on filial piety and family harmony, which can add layers of complexity to the experience of maternal absence. Women may grapple with feelings of guilt or obligation while striving to fulfill societal expectations and navigating the emotional terrain of their own experiences. Maternal absence, while challenging, can also be a catalyst for growth and self-discovery, prompting women to redefine motherhood in ways that honor their experiences and aspirations. By acknowledging and understanding these diverse perspectives, we can cultivate a more empathetic and inclusive understanding of motherhood within Asian-American cultures and beyond.

Reflection Questions

1. What do you consider your ethnicity or social class to be? How is your perspective of what a mom is influenced by your ethnicity or your social class?
2. How do you think that the role of a mother differs between your mother and your maternal grandmother?

CHAPTER 4
MALE PERSPECTIVES ON MOTHERHOOD:
ROLE FOR SONS

The role of motherhood, upon which many women reflect a great deal, also attracts the interest and consideration of males. Men have a unique perspective on motherhood despite not having the experience of being mothers themselves. This perspective is shaped by their connections with their own mothers, spouses, and children, as well as by cultural conventions and personal convictions.

Many men associate motherhood with care, compassion, and selflessness. Their conception of motherhood is based on their observations of the commitment and sacrifices that their mothers made for the welfare of their family. Because they understand how important these sacrifices are to the fabric of family life, men frequently appreciate and admire the effort that women put into raising their children.

In addition to their own experiences, men are influenced by the opinions of other people about what a mother should be. Role models that they encounter directly or indirectly also help shape men's views on motherhood. As women work through the difficulties of motherhood together and men see their partners' successes, struggles, and strengths as mothers, these men and women could find encouragement in one another. Men's perspectives can also be influenced and reflected by how society portrays mothers in literature, in the media, and in cultural narratives. Popular culture contains many portrayals of ideal or flawed mothers (as well as of women in general) through such things as movies, television shows, and advertisements. These portrayals of mothers can influence men's views of what mothers should be like.

The views of men on motherhood provide important insights into the complexity of family life and the varied nature of parental responsibilities and expectations. Even though men are not mothers, men's views, experiences, and thoughts help us comprehend the crucial roles that women play in influencing the lives of their children and families.

What is the role of the mother for her sons? How important is the mother–son relationship? Surprisingly and unfortunately, only limited recent research has explored the mother–son relationship. This fact is troubling, considering how many women are raising sons alone. Just as it is for the mother–daughter relationship, the role of a mother in her son's life is also viewed through a subjective lens and is influenced by multiple variables: personal, familial, cultural, and societal.

Some would say that the mother helps the son to develop the ability to nurture by the way she shows her love to him through her actions. Some would say that the nurturing that he needs in his earlier years is more likely to be given by his mother than his father. This nurturing helps him to develop a positive sense of self. Some men believe that the mother is the familial matriarch and the foundation of the family. This is the case for Eric, a 60-year-old African-American male, who stated,

> "Moms provide love, guidance, and nurturing. [The mom is] the leader of the home, the peacemaker, [and] the stabilizer of the family. [She is] the head of the 'village.' What I learned from my mom is patience, structure, how to survive, humility, and how to care for others when it's hard. She is the anchor of the family because she teaches empathy, understanding, and coaching and can provide the balance required in the familial unit."

Eric's developed what he described as an anxious attachment to his mother. He was the third of four children and described himself as the invisible one (what others sometimes call the lost or forgotten child). He reported that his mother was his protector from his verbally abusive and neglectful father. The father's disposition differed from the mother's, so what Eric experienced with his father was also different. The impact of his mother's parenting seems to be reflected in Eric's current behavior. He tends to be structured, controlling, super-independent, and distrustful of others. Perhaps Eric's disclosure was about the idealized mother he desired.

Miguel, a 40-year-old Hispanic male, has had an experience with some similarities to Eric's, as both perceive the mother as the backbone of the family, providing strength and being its matriarch. She is the one who is relied on for both emotional and physical needs. Miguel stated,

> "I was raised by my grandmother because my biological father and mother both abandoned me. I consider my grand-

mother my mom. She provided food, shelter, and love. Tough love. She did not want me to grow up to be a punk, or soft, or a sissy, but I . . . started hanging with the wrong crowd. When I got in trouble, she did not bail me out. Instead, I had to deal with the consequences of whatever stupid choices I made.

"I even went to juvenile detention. but no matter what I did, her love remained, and I know that her love was unconditional. The knowledge of that and the unintentional testing of her love and the results of that testing are what made me straighten up my life. My grandmother's [role], or should I say my mom's role, was to . . . provide unwavering unconditional love and support, even when the kids fuck up."

It is not uncommon for men of color who are raised by extended family such and grandparents to grow up and mature fast—even if this is sometimes through trial and error. But it appeared that Miguel's knowledge that his grandmother's love would not end, that he would not be abandoned by her, and the need to honor her may have helped Miguel to find his way. However, he did indicate that he struggles with abandonment issues. These manifested as an anxious-preoccupied attachment style in his current marriage. He is aware of its origin. He stated that he does not believe that this is due to his grandmother, the one he calls "Mom," the one who raised him. Instead, this insecure attachment style is the result of the unanswered questions he has of the biological mother who bore him. He has never met her.

Frank, a 55-year-old biracial male, said,

"It's obvious that a mom's job is to nurture and protect. She carries the kid for nine months, [which is] where her protection of her child starts, right? Well, my mother had a hard time protecting herself from my abusive father, so who protected me? No one but me. In fact, I got molested as a 12-year-old after running away from home.

"It was like I was born to be in survival mode, born to care for myself. . . . I was not really nurtured by my mother the way I believed that a mother should nurture, but I also understand why. Nonetheless, it still affected me a lot—as I, yes, I am about to say this, and some may think I sound like a woman. But I went on a quest for love. There was a deep hunger for the nurturing that I did not receive as a child. I craved it—like a child starving for nourishment.

"I found myself hitting adulthood with a huge void. It was a mother void, so I found myself going from one relationship to another. Not just any relationship—but a marital relationship—one after the other. At some point in each marriage, the void was recreated. It was that same void I felt as a child, but I never understood why.

"I was married three times, and now that I am single, I hope that I meet my last one, the one till death do us part. I have done a lot of work on myself. I have worked to heal my anxious-preoccupied attachment style, and now I am not afraid to be alone like before. I now have a secure attachment to God first and many good lifelong friends."

Frank's experience is bittersweet. While it is phenomenal to hear how he has overcome traumas from the past, one of which was the lack of nurturing from his mother, his struggle and the pain he experienced in his journey are heartbreaking. Perhaps he was searching in the eyes of his wives for the mother that the younger wounded part of him needed.

Sorrento's experience was similar. Sorrento, a 68-year-old white man, stated, "Growing up in a home with alcoholism and violence as a child, [I found that] my mother was my protector. From an early age, my father was consistently in and out of our lives. It was during the upheavals of my childhood that my mother was the parent who battled to keep us safe. My mother was not exempt from the effects of an alcoholic husband, nor the utter fear of what violence might await her day or night. In essence, I became an anxious adult version of my childhood experiences."

When I asked Sorrento what he needed from his mother, he stated, "At one time, I needed approval. My mother and sister are enmeshed. Before I understood their enmeshment as a trauma bond, I had made it about me."

Although Sorrento did not always get what he needed, he did reflect on the positive things that he did get from his mother: "She taught me to keep going. Even if it was on my hands and knees, keep going." He reflected on the wisdom that he had gained on his healing journey from therapy, several romantic relationships, his mother, and overall childhood experiences:

> "Many years ago, my sister, my mother, and [I] made a day journey to her childhood roots. I found my mother to be what each of us is, simply a human being, one who was shaped and created by influences that in some cases are as relevant today as they were the day they happened. My mother has done the best she could with the knowledge and insight she has. This is true of all of humanity since the beginning of time.
>
> "As I have peeled back the layers of the onion of my life, I found sharing my journey to be far more difficult for the

listening party. I have found a good chance that the listening party has yet to come to terms with their own root issues, so it isn't too long before something has been triggered. I believe that all of us share in the same common frailties of mankind, past, present, and future.

"There are clearly variables in each life experience, and certainly there are outliers, but . . . we are simply taking turns at experiencing this thing called our existence. As I have grown wiser, I am more accepting of Christ's words at the Cross when he said, 'Forgive them, Father, for they know what not they do.' "

Some of the roles of mothers identified by men were:

- teaching values
- cooking meals
- nurturing kids when they get hurt
- protecting kids from harm
- providing clothing and school support
- keeping the dad in line
- running the household
- resolving problems at the kid's school
- being a doctor or nurse
- tutoring
- resolving conflicts.

Reflection Questions

1. What did your mother teach you that you feel is important to you as a man?

2. In what ways do you feel that the way you interact with women is affected by what you saw in your mother growing up?
3. How did your relationship with her help shape the man that you are today?

CHAPTER 5
MEN'S ETHNIC AND CULTURAL
PERSPECTIVES OF MOTHERHOOD

Perspective of Male African Americans

In the African-American community, discussions about maternal roles carry profound significance, often reflecting complex historical legacies and contemporary social realities. Traditionally, maternal figures have played a central role in African-American families, providing emotional support, guidance, and strength in the face of adversity. Mothers are often revered as pillars of the community, embodying qualities of resilience, sacrifice, and unconditional love. Their influence extends beyond the confines of the home, shaping the values and aspirations of future generations. For African-American men, the presence of a nurturing and supportive maternal figure can be transformative, instilling a sense of self-worth and belonging that reverberates throughout their lives. Whether it's a mother, a grandmother, an aunt, or another maternal figure, their guidance serves as a beacon of hope amid societal challenges and systemic injustices.

DR. SHARON BATY

Perspective of Male Anglos

Traditionally, motherhood has been closely associated with femininity and seen as the primary domain of women. The mother traditionally plays the supportive role in the heterosexual relationship. She is often the one responsible for caring for the kids' emotional needs, planning extracurricular activities, and providing nourishment through consistent daily meal planning and preparation.

Perspective of Male Native Americans: Maternal Structures and Tribal Perspectives

The idea of motherhood is closely linked to cultural values, family dynamics, and ancestral practices in Native-American societies.

Mothers have an important and highly valued role in the health of many Native-American communities. Mothers are frequently viewed as the primary carers, imparting cultural values, transferring ancestors' wisdom, and tending to the next generation. On the other hand, a mother's lack of involvement or neglect of her children can have detrimental effects on the entire family and on the broader tribal community.

Perspective of Male Asian Americans

Historically, traditional Asian societies have often placed a strong emphasis on the role of mothers as nurturers and caregivers within the family. Motherhood is revered and regarded as a sacred duty, with mothers esteemed for their selflessness, sacrifice, and unwavering dedication to their children's wellbeing. In these societies, men typically hold a deep respect for the maternal figure, viewing motherhood as the cornerstone of family harmony and societal stability.

Summary

Men who grow up in these kinds of settings might absorb these conventional beliefs and regard parenthood as a holy and necessary institution. By giving their mothers and future spouses steadfast support through the ups and downs of parenting, they may hope to maintain the values of filial piety and honor. Men are often expected to play the roles of guardians and providers, while women are largely in charge of nurturing and providing care, according to traditional gender norms. Because of this, men's views on motherhood may be heavily influenced by their responsibilities as sons, husbands, and dads, with a focus on obligations to their families.

Reflection Questions

1. How is your perspective of what a mom is supposed to be influenced by your ethnicity or your social class? For example, what are the gender role expectations of a mother according to your culture, social background, or ethnicity?
2. In your adult relationships, how do these expectations manifest? How are they challenged?

CHAPTER 6
LEARNING MOTHERHOOD BY PROXY-BREAKING UNINTENTIONALLY

Mothers learn to be mothers by how they are mothered. It is not uncommon for a mother to become the carbon copy of her own mother, whether her mother was a positive and healthy mother or an unhealthy one. When they become mothers, many women may choose to become the opposite of what they experienced, especially if they grew up with a mother who was unhealthy in some manner (e.g., mentally ill, abusive, or absent).

Hollywood may create pressure for some mothers as they could get their main ideas about motherhood from watching sitcoms and movies. Many of these fictional mother figures seem close to perfection. Such mothers include but are not limited to Florida Evans, played by Esther Rolle in the 1970s sitcom *Good Times*. Emerging as the rational, wise familial matriarch, her role as a mother was a powerful example of what a mother could be. Another example is Carol Brady, played by Florence Henderson in the sitcom *The Brady Bunch*. Carol Brady played the role of the family's nurturing, practical mediator and rational problem solver. Her character was relatable and down-to-earth. She seemed to make the role of mother and stepmother effortless and enjoyable.

While these examples of mothers in two very different sitcoms send a strong and concise message of what the role of a mother is or may be, it is fair to say that although these fictional families may look similar to real families, they are not real families, and the children who play the roles of their children are not the parents' biological offspring. Motherhood may look like the experiences of Carol Brady and Florida Evan's on some days, but on other days, mothers' roles in their kids' lives and the way they resolve issues on the set don't always reflect what actually happens most of the time in the real world. Some mothers struggle with mothering. What it means to be a mother may be different based on culture, the developmental age of the mother, trauma, mental illness, and substance abuse, among many other factors.

Hollywood does not always acknowledge the reality of the challenges of being a mother. If the relationship of the mother and daughter is damaged due to neglect, abuse, absenteeism, substance abuse, or mental illness, and healing doesn't take place for the daughter or the mother, it's not uncommon for the daughter later in her life to struggle with navigating motherhood with her own children.

If understanding this unfortunate phenomenon of the effects of unhealthy mothering is sought, it's important to seek to understand it without excusing any lack of healthy mothering. The best way to start is to ask questions of the mother about her childhood relationship with her own mother. Learning about the type of relationship between the mother and her mother or mother figure can be essential in the healing process.

I asked a few women, "Where did you learn about what it means to be a mother?" Audrey, a 32-year-old mother of four, stated,

> "My mother used to yell and scream. She used to beat us. When she wasn't beating us, she would ignore us. She did this until the authorities removed us from her home. We were in foster care for a while—until my grandmother got us. My grandmother didn't hurt us as much, but she was strict. If any of us had a problem, she told us to figure it out before asking for help.
>
> "Now, as a mother, I yell, scream, and cuss a lot. I don't like to be touched, and I don't always show compassion towards my kids. I want to work on being more understanding, but it's hard. What I think makes a good mom is someone who sacrifices, compromises, and provides assurance for kids with the other parent."

As Audrey made her disclosure, tears welled up in her eyes as she realized that some of her current negative mothering behaviors are a mix of what she witnessed and received from her biological mother and her grandmother. She did, however, recognize the need to break the cycle that seems to be repeating in her own mothering of her children. She admits that she is open and realizes that she does need some help with parenting. She did report having a desire to give her kids what she did not receive, but it's easier to revert to unconsciously learned behaviors from childhood.

Tracie, a 45-year-old single mother, stated,

> "I never desired to be a single mother—a mother, yes—but not a single mother. I am raising two boys and two girls. I

was married when I had them—and it was easier with two parents raising kids.

"But I divorced [their dad] because he was a cheater, and he was abusive. . . . Sometimes I wish I had never had them, at least with the man I chose, because I am damn tired of motherhood, especially when they act up. I admit that I can be controlling with them and have very little patience.

"I will never be like the mom I had. She gave us up to the foster care system. She hated being a mom too. Her mother—my grandmother—was abusive. She was critical, condescending, and mean. I guess that as much as I despise her, maybe I am her. You will be happy to know that I am taking parenting classes, and I am doing the best that I can."

The mother who takes on the role of both parents is a superhero to some—but some mothers may not feel that way about themselves. That is the case for Tracie. Her mother's inability to mother her appears to have influenced her mothering of her own kids. She appears to be struggling with understanding what a mother is supposed to be—other than being a provider, which Tracie is. But is she playing that role out of obligation or guilt? When she was asked, her answer was, "Both."

If the mother was broken by her mother due to abuse, neglect, absenteeism, substance abuse, or mental illness and she does not seek help to heal, she may unintentionally break her own children. The broken and unhealed child then grows up to be a broken adult, and the cycle of brokenness or trauma continues.

What does it mean to be broken? When children are mothered by a mom who is broken due the issues just mentioned, they may become fragmented and damaged due to their unfulfilled needs.

They may develop an unhealthy insecure attachment style or any number of other mental-health issues.

Reflection Questions

1. What mistakes do you believe that your mother made when she was mothering you?
2. From what you know about your mother's childhood, what do you think may have influenced the way that she mothered you?
3. Describe the relationship your mother had with her mother (your maternal grandmother). What did you observe?

CHAPTER 7
ATTACHMENT TRAUMA:
BROKEN CHILD MANIFESTATION

Attachment trauma may result when a mother ignores or dismisses a child's needs, as evidenced by neglect of the baby's needs, such as failure to provide consistent nourishment, affection, care, or comfort. However, attachment trauma can arise throughout the child's development. Due to various factors, some mothers do not respond to their children's needs. Many kids survive by developing coping behaviors that seem to be a manifestation of attachment trauma. Those experiences in early life with caregivers can determine whether a child develops an avoidant, an anxious, or a disorganized attachment. These attachment styles influence how an individual starts and maintains relationships.

These manifestations of attachment trauma may result in insecure attachment styles (anxious, avoidant, and disorganized) and may lead to many other issues. These attachment styles may directly affect the way the adult child responds to her or his own child or other adults. Those who do not become parents may struggle to develop healthy attachments in relationships with friends, romantic partners, siblings, and authority figures (e.g., bosses). In the following section, these insecure attachment styles are defined and examined within the context of the cases presented above.

Anxious, Avoidant, and Disorganized or Insecure Attachment Styles

What does a person with an avoidant (dismissive) attachment style look like? Avoidant individuals try to avoid closeness with others and emotional intimacy. They tend to downgrade the importance of relationships, not to express feelings, and to maintain independence so as not to be trapped in any position that would put them in a state of being vulnerable. This attachment style usually develops when that person's caregivers have been unresponsive or emotionally unavailable. Use the check-list below to evaluate yourself. Check each statement that applies to you.

___ I struggle with closeness and intimacy.
___ I keep my friends or my partner at a distance.
___ I don't want to get too close due to my need to be in control.
___ I am afraid of being betrayed again.
___ I am mistrustful of others.
___ I have difficulty being open and vulnerable.
___ I have been (or I am) unfaithful; I have had numerous sexual conquests or am uncomfortable with labeling a relationship as monogamous or committed.
___ I sometimes feel as though my partner is too clingy.
___ I withdraw and cope with difficult situations alone.
___ I suppress my emotions or push emotions down.

___ I shut down easily.

Taya, a 43-year-old biracial woman, stated,

"I immediately became avoidant dismissive [in my] attachment [style] because of the fear that what happened to my mother would happen to me [if I got] close to a man. . . . I think that she intentionally taught me not to trust men and always to have the means to take care of myself. It's hard for me to commit to one man. If I do decide to get in a relationship, it's on my terms. I'm petrified of being betrayed the way my mom was.

"I have a difficult time being open and vulnerable with anybody. I am super-independent. Like I mentioned earlier, my mother didn't know any better. She grew up in a different time. At the time she met my father, once you got knocked up, you would get married, whether you loved the person or not, so she married a man who didn't respect her. He married her out of duty as a man who grew up in the South in the 1950s. My attachment style isn't directly related to something my mom did not give me relative to nurturing and care. It is what she taught me through her actions while I was growing up."

Taya believed her mom to be a nurturer. Taya even described her attachment to her mother as very secure, but her attachment issues in adulthood result from what she talked about earlier: her mom's failure to teach Taya what it means to be female and a wife.

What does the anxiously (preoccupied) attached person look like? Anxious individuals desire a high level of closeness and approval from their partner; however, they fear being rejected or abandoned.

They may be hyper-vigilant about relationship cues, seeking reassurance and fearing abandonment. Such anxious attachment can result from inconsistent caregiving, wherein caregivers are sometimes nurturing and sometimes neglectful. Use the checklist below to evaluate yourself, checking each statement that is true for you:

___ I need constant emotional reassurance.
___ I want to be with my partner all the time.
___ I feel hyper-vigilant (on edge) about the relationship.
___ I worry about my worthiness in a relationship, asking myself, "Am I good enough?"
___ I worry my partner's desire to be with me. (For example, I ask myself, "Will he [or she] leave me? What will I do?")
___ I hope that my partner will rescue or complete me.
___ I feel desperate.
___ I feel insecure in the relationship.
___ I am demanding of my partner.
___ I feel possessive, jealous, or controlling toward my partner.
___ I often interpret my partner's actions as being rejecting or insensitive, even if they aren't.

Teresa, a 30-year-old, stated,

"I don't remember everything in my childhood, but a lot of people from outside, like my uncles and even my dad, said that my mom treated me really badly. I think she was jealous of the relationship me and my dad had. I would go and talk to my dad instead of my mom. But it was not like we didn't have food or that our basic needs were not met. She did do a lot of things that were good. We went on vacations to Disneyland [or other places] every summer. I had horses, a pool, and all that kind of stuff.

"But my mom was emotionally absent. This absence became more pronounced after my mom and dad got divorced. She was terrible to me. It was like she punished me after my dad was gone, especially when I would cry because I missed my dad. She would tell me to shut up and stop crying because she did not want to hear it. She took her anger out on me. Everything was always my fault. She was always mad at me, but then she treated my brother completely different. He was her favorite.

"I think I became indifferent at first, acting out, drinking, running away—and then I discovered boys—and that was when I think I started struggling with my self-esteem and hated being alone. I just wanted to be loved. I was very insecure. I was very jealous and controlling. I started to wonder whether I was good enough and whether my boyfriend was gonna leave me.

"When I got pregnant with my first child, I felt like that was an insurance policy that I would finally have the family that I desired, but boy, was I wrong! When that relationship ended, I jumped right into another one, and I kept on being mistreated. I wondered, 'Why now as a 30-year-old?' I think that I was looking to a boyfriend for the love I felt from my father. Not in a weird way. I just wanted to be loved and nurtured. Maybe it was the little girl in me that just wanted somebody to be there forever."

What does the disorganized attached person look like? A person with a disorganized attachment may behave unpredictably, fear closeness while longing for it, and be unable to modulate emotions. Typically, disorganized attachment results from abusive, traumatic, or extremely inconsistent caregiving experiences. It can look like a combination of anxious and avoidant attachment styles. Often, this may be the result of growing up with a mentally ill mother or other caregiver (often a mental illness that comes with unstable moods). These mood changes are highly unpredictable. Examples of illnesses with an unstable mood component are: bipolar disorder, substance abuse, and major depressive disorders. Use the checklist below to evaluate yourself. Check each statement that applies to you.

___ I am consumed with fear about closeness.
___ I push and pull in relationships, saying things like this: "You can go! Wait! I didn't mean it. Please don't leave!"
___ I feel intense loneliness and shame, which affects my self-esteem, so I may hang onto an unhealthy relationship due to worry about what others will think.
___ I talk negative about myself, criticizing myself as a partner.
___ I may have trouble regulating my mood. I get triggered easily and become reactive, which affects my relationship.
___ I sometime start fights.
___ I look for signs of infidelity in my partner that may not be there.
___ If a breakup occurs, I shut down and convince myself that I never even liked my partner in the first place.
___ I push my partner and say things impulsively that could ruin the relationship.

Sally reflected on her experience with her mom, stating that her mom's influence on her was significant (but was impacted by the early loss of her mother). Sally stated, "I am very giving and loving but also can be anxious and avoidant with others, sometimes isolating myself as an adult."

Sally identified the attachment style she struggles with as disorganized attachment, stating, "I showed up as the unhealed inner child." Sally may have been allowing her wounded inner child to choose her partners. What does this mean? All the unmet needs of the wounded little girl rise to the surface. After a relationship has ended, we may judge and criticize our actions. In essence, we are judging the wounded inner self. For Sally, that wounded inner self might be about 10 years old. The book *I am Me: Embracing all Aspects of the True Self: The Self-Integration Theory of Healing* explores the process of healing the younger versions of self. It focuses on giving the younger self a voice so that healing can take place.

Sally did, however, identify keeping people at an arm's distance unless she needs to be vulnerable, which involves someone with whom she has built trust. This keeping people at an arm's distance may give Sally the illusion of control so she does not get hurt or feel abandoned. This makes sense because her illusion of control helps her avoid pain to her younger inner self.

Victoria, who also identified as disorganized attached, was asked how she shows up in relationships. She stated,

"Kimberly is my fiancé. We [will] get married in September and have been together for two years now. I wonder sometimes if I'm dreaming. I'm like, "She's putting up with me? What does she see in me?" I feel like all my past childhood trauma of being critical of myself is appearing on the surface more and more. I don't know how to handle it.

"I love Kimberly so much that I worry that it will scare her away. I worry that I will say something mean and that she'll be gone like a puff of smoke. I look at her sometimes and must rub my eyes because I can't believe she's real and sitting right next to me. I remind myself that I am worthy of love.

"There are times, though, when we don't have sex that [I think that] something is wrong with me. That dark voice of mine in my head says, 'She's cheating on you. You better lose weight. You're ugly.'

"I am my own punching bag, and I pelt myself with a hailstorm of self-hatred. I struggle to love myself. I wonder, 'What did these women see in me?' I would often use my body to sell myself, so to speak. I didn't have any respect for myself because I thought the women I dated wanted only my body, not my heart, soul, or intelligence."

Victoria appeared to try to make sense out of her mom's behavior towards her. She surmised that her mother was closer to Victoria's maternal grandfather. She described her maternal grandmother as critical of her mother, always concerned about the opinions of others outside the home. Victoria stated,

"My mom struggled with drug addiction. My dad told me one time that my grandma (my mom's mom) said, 'I have three daughters. One is perfect, one is a drug addict, and one is a slut.' My mom was the middle child out of three girls, the one who struggled with the drugs. She was the black sheep of the family. She was always treated [badly]."

Victoria's mom did not know how to mother except in the way that she was treated by her own mother. Perhaps Victoria's mom projected her anger towards her own mother onto Victoria. Victoria stated,

"I am very anxious and avoidant. This has played a strong role in my relationships because I think I'm never good enough. I don't see myself as beautiful because my mom always used to criticize my weight when I was a teenager. I associated my not wearing makeup, being overweight, being a tomboy, and having braces with being ugly. I don't remember my mom telling me that I was beautiful. Today, I am 33 years old, and I am terrified of gaining weight. One pound over on the scale could fuck up my day."

Victoria also reflected on experiences of infidelity perpetrated by male and female romantic partners that have played a role in shaping her identity. One relationship with a female affected her the most. Victoria stated,

"I correlated her bad behavior to what my mom would say about my looks—for example, that I wasn't good enough. I want to say I have gotten better. There are times when I bury these negative emotions and memories so deep that I explode. I start throwing and punching things, cutting up my arms and stomach, and screaming."

Victoria described the disclosure of this experience as cathartic. She does recognize that she still needs healing but has recognized the root of her attachment trauma.

Attachment styles affect relational dynamics, communication patterns, and emotional responses. Understanding one's attachment style can help create healthier relationships through therapy and personal reflection. For example, learning new relational skills can help someone to develop a secure attachment based on trust, consistency, and emotional presence.

Reflection Questions

1. If you believe that you have an insecure attachment style, which one do you most align with?
2. Why do you believe that you developed that insecure attachment style?
3. How does that specific attachment style affect your friendships and romantic relationships?
4. As an adult, how do you feel about your attachment to your mother?

CHAPTER 8
TYPES OF MOTHERS

Imagine the countless ways in which a mother's actions influence her child's life. Her actions include more than just providing necessities; they are an intricate web of interactions and caregiving practices. These are what we call maternal behaviors. They are the foundation of the strong bond between mother and child.

Maternal behaviors come in many forms. There's the comforting hug after a scrape, the firm but loving discipline that teaches right from wrong, the gentle touch, the playful laughter shared during a game, and the encouraging words whispered before a big test. These seemingly simple moments hold immense power. They shape the child's emotional development, sense of self-worth, and overall wellbeing.

The way a mother parents—her unique blend of nurturing, affection, and guidance—can have a great and lasting impact on her child. It can influence a child's ability to review the world, build healthy relationships, and cope with challenges. By understanding these diverse maternal behaviors, we can gain valuable insights into the complex dynamics of the mother–child bond and how it shapes a child's life journey.

This understanding isn't just about acknowledging the greatness of mothers. It's also about recognizing the bond between a mother and her child. It's about the countless ways that these behaviors, big and small, influence the core of who a child becomes.

Some children get blessed with the mother that they need or want. As mentioned before, a lot of who the mother becomes is related to how she was mothered or nurtured. She often learns what it means to be a mother by what she experiences from her own mother. We know, however, that this isn't always the case. Some mothers grow up in an abusive environment with an abusive or absent mother yet still become good mothers to their own children later. This is not uncommon, but some would say it's more likely that she will repeat the same negative pattern of mothering if she does not heal from what she experienced from her own mother.

In the next section, the types of unhealthy mothers will be discussed:

- the arrested-development mother
- the abusive mother
- the uninvolved and neglectful mother
- the mentally ill mother.

The Arrested-Development Mother

The arrested-developed mother is permissive and often wants to play the role of a friend rather than that of a parent. She is indulgent, often allowing her children a great deal of freedom to explore and make decisions on their own even before they are old enough.

She's often lenient with her rules and doesn't set clear boundaries between herself and her children. She may not place many restrictions or limitations on her kids.

In their interactions with their kids, such a mother may communicate and behave in a childlike manner that is not congruent with her chronological age. She may come across as dependent and even anxious. She may display passivity with her kids when problems surface. She may struggle with difficulties, avoiding making decisions that are best for her children and herself. She may come across as avoidant of conflict, often resorting to people-pleasing.

The indulgent mother's behaviors result in the kids feeling that they're in control because their mother has a difficult time saying no. This is often due to the mother's extreme fear of being abandoned or being disliked by her children. In essence, she wants to be her kids' friend. Behaviors such as these are consistent with dependent personality disorder.

In addition, such a mother may show unstable moods, veering from extreme euphoria to angry outbursts. She may struggle with intermittent impulses to harm herself or to commit suicide. She is the mother who has a hard time being alone, so she may go from one relationship to another. She may constantly talk negatively about herself, putting herself down frequently. She may thrive on getting validation about her worthiness from her kids and her partners. She may talk to her kids about her relationship challenges. These mothers often treat their daughters like girlfriends and sons like pseudo-husbands. Behaviors such as these are consistent with borderline personality disorder.

These mothers may also feel that they are in competition with their daughters for attention from males. Such mothers may dress provocatively and want to hang out with their daughters' friends because they identify with people much younger than they are.

They are reactive when given feedback by their daughters and have a hard time taking responsibility for the emotional pain that they cause her kids or others as they struggle with empathizing with the feelings of others. If these mothers attempt to empathize, such efforts may be inauthentic and exaggerated, especially when others are watching. These mothers get frustrated easily if others don't notice every positive effort they make to improve their behavior as mothers.

Such mothers may show up as codependent, although unfortunately, there is still no universally accepted diagnosis for codependency. What is known about codependency is that it takes place when an individual's self-worth and identity are wrapped around being a rescuer of other people. In this case, the mother's self-worth is tied to the responsibilities of being a caregiver to her child, but the codependent mother often expects her children to do something in return to validate her care of them.

The codependent person looks like a martyr who endures the pain inflicted on her caused by other people. Either she makes excuses for it or believes that it's her job to suffer. This relational dynamic is one in which one person relies excessively upon another person for emotional support, validation, or self-esteem. This relationship dynamic may be seen in the mother.

Kids raised by mothers with arrested development might struggle with:

- controlling impulses
- exercising self-discipline
- setting appropriate boundaries in relationships
- showing respect for authority figures
- taking on parentified behaviors as children
- having volatile moods

- developing healthy self-esteem
- trusting others
- forming healthy adult attachments
- behaving playfully rather than always being serious
- needing to be in control all or most of the time

The Abusive Mother

The abusive mother may be emotionally, physically, or sexually abusive to her children. She is known for her strictness and her need for control, obedience, rigidity, and conformity. She sets inflexible rules and high expectations. Sometimes she enforces discipline through extreme punishment and coercion. The old saying "children should be seen and not heard" implies that adults are the authority on everything and that children should never question adults' authority. Instead, children should simply comply. Abusive mothers often struggle with emotional connection and empathy. These mothers often see their kids as objects or property that may sometimes be used for the mother's benefit. The mother's abusive behavior and lack of patience communicates a negative message to her kids about their value.

The abuse that the mother may display may be used to exploit her kids or to manipulate them. She may display explosive violence and angry behavior. She may hurt her kids without concern or regret. She may have a hard time taking responsibility or showing remorse for harming her children. If she assaults them physically or verbally in a fit of anger, she may apologize but then negate the apology by telling them that they caused her to behave that way: "Look what you made me do!"

The mother may even lose custody of her kids due to her abuse of them or due to the choices she makes or forces the kids to make that violate the law. For example, she may have the kids steal or commit other crimes. She may hurt them or guilt trip them in some way if they refuse. These behaviors are consistent with antisocial personality disorder.

Some mothers guilt trip the kids about how lucky they are to have such a mother. Such a mother seeks to obtain admiration from her kids regarding who she is. She may often compare herself to other mothers, highlighting how she is superior. She may dismiss the needs of her children, prioritizing her own needs and struggling to empathize with her kids' feelings.

If her kids or other people want to give her feedback about what she's doing wrong or what they need, she often has a hard time acknowledging anything negative about herself, so she may make the kids believe that whatever issues they have is a result of something that they have done wrong. She often sees herself as more important than her kids and will continually put her own needs before the needs of her kids. These behaviors are consistent with narcissistic personality disorder.

Children raised by abusive mothers may exhibit:

- elevated levels of anxiety
- low self-esteem
- difficulty expressing their emotions
- outbursts of anger
- volatile moods
- difficulties with authority figures
- substance abuse
- excessive risk-taking behaviors
- mental illness
- delinquent behavior in adolescence and adulthood

The Uninvolved and Neglectful Mother

An uninvolved or neglectful mother is emotionally detached and disengaged from her child's life, often due to personal issues or external stressors. She may neglect her child's physical and emotional needs, providing only minimal supervision, guidance, or support. These mothers may struggle with challenges that interfere with their ability to parent effectively. These mothers may be physically or emotionally absent from their kids' lives. Some mothers will choose to resign from their job as a mother and leave the other parent to raise the children, from then on having little or no contact with them.

Sometimes these mothers are physically there but emotionally absent. They are usually distracted by other things, such as relationships, social media, jobs, other social roles, and activities. Mothering is a low priority.

Mothers' emotional detachment might result from drug abuse or extreme stress brought on by circumstances such as financial difficulties (poverty or financial setbacks). A mother facing the stress of financial instability might be so focused on survival that she inadvertently neglects her child's emotional needs.

Uninvolved mothers rarely show up for teachers' conferences or for their kids' performances or extracurricular activities. These mothers may consistently make promises that they fail to keep. These mothers can be at social class extremes. Some of these mothers can be substance abusers, whereas others may be CEOs of Fortune 500 companies. The neglect of their children is not always conscious or intentional; many of these mothers may love their children and may show that love by indulging their kids financially to compensate for their absence or neglect. These mothers' detachment and emotional unavailability can have detrimental effects on a child's wellbeing and growth.

Children raised by uninvolved mothers may experience insecure attachment, substance abuse, and feelings of:

- abandonment
- insecurity
- anger
- depression
- anxiety, which can be extreme

The Mentally Ill Mother

The mother who struggles with mental illness has her own set of challenges. Whether her mental illness is a result of genetic predisposition, trauma, or circumstances beyond her control, mothering while navigating the symptoms of the mental illness can be very difficult. This is especially true when the mental illness is not being treated.

Some mothers struggle with mood disorders, such as bi-polar or major depressive disorder. Some suffer from a trauma-related disorder, such as post-traumatic stress disorder (PTSD) or anxiety. Others chronically abuse substances. Some have a psychotic disorder, such as schizophrenia. Whatever the cause or form of the mother's mood disorder, it is hard on the child because he or she may find himself or herself having to grow up too fast to be able to take care of themselves, their younger siblings, and perhaps even the mother herself.

With many mentally ill mothers, unpredictability goes along with their interactions with their children. If the mother is seen as the one who creates a foundation for safe and secure attachment but her behavior and interactions with her kids are unpredictable, this imbalance between duty and performance can create a tentativeness or uncertainty in the child.

This tentativeness or uncertainty in children can manifest in different ways. The child may begin experiencing mental-health symptoms at an early age. This may not be due to genetic predisposition as much as exposure to unsafe living conditions. These children may experience various issues throughout their early life and adulthood, which is the subject of the following chapter.

Reflection Questions

1. Which type of mother do you feel that you had?
2. In what ways were you able to see your mother as she was when you were a child?
3. In what ways were you in denial about your mother when you were a child? In what ways was that denial helpful? Harmful?
4. How did your view of her change in adolescence and adulthood?
5. How did having that type of mother affect you as a child? As an adolescence? As an adult?

CHAPTER 9
THE ADULT CHILD:
PARENTIFIED BEHAVIORS

Parentified behavior may be seen in children who have a neglectful or uninvolved mother. The parentified child acts like a parent to his or her own parents or siblings. Some of the most common causes identified as possible reasons behind such behavior include illness in the family, financial problems, or just having an emotionally unavailable parent.

Children who play these roles regularly take care of the home, offer emotional support to others in the family, or even work to generate money. In doing so, although taking on such roles and responsibilities at an early age may help develop skills such as empathy, accountability, self-reliance, and independence, this can come at a cost: The children often forfeit their childhood experiences, which may then lead to depression, anxiety, or resentment.

Long-term effects may include trouble setting healthy limits or forming boundaries in healthy relationships. The parentified child can carry excessive responsibility or guilt, along with a proneness to excessive self-criticism and harsh self-judgment. Parentified children can continue to succumb to caring for others' needs instead of their own. They may neglect self-care and may find it hard to stand up for themselves even as adults.

The parentified behaviors of the adult child discussed in this chapter include:

- perfectionism
- problems with conduct and anger
- substance abuse
- self-mutilation
- running away from home
- eating disorders

Perfectionism

Some kids develop perfectionism. This often results from experiences in which they may have been abused verbally or physically. The pursuit of flawlessness and setting high performance standards may have been a way for the child to avoid being hurt. They may have promised to offer the chance to gain some recognition, however fleeting or illusory. Although some may have found such a trait as a motivating factor in success, it may have also created feelings of anxiety, worry, and fear of failure. The expectation of commendation and appreciation from others may put extra pressure on them as they may dread making mistakes. Perfectionists also tend to be overly critical of themselves and others.

Perfectionism can play out in in adult relationships. Adult children tend to have very high expectations of their partners. Such high expectations may manifest as controlling behavior imposed on the partner, which can create disputes and ongoing tensions in a relationship.

This perfectionism can also affect how the adult child parents his or her own kids. However unintentionally, the perfectionistic adult child can create the same type of distress and anxiety in their own kids as they experienced growing up. Breaking the generational cycle of perfectionism requires becoming aware of the pattern and making choices to diminish its grip.

Problems with Conduct and Anger

In addition to perfectionism, conduct and anger problems may develop. These problems can denote sustained patterns of aggressive or disruptive behaviors in individuals. Such behaviors can persist from childhood through adolescence and into adulthood. In childhood and adolescence, oppositional defiance and hostility towards authority figures may manifest in response to suffering from the experiences that a child has in the home environment from having a neglectful or an abusive mother.

The inability to control the anger that these children might experience may be due to the explosion of the suppressed negative emotions. These emotions may not have been safe to express as a child. If not addressed, this anger and defiant behavior can spill over to the adult child's interactions with his or her own kids.

Substance Abuse

Substance abuse is another problem that can manifest in response to trauma experienced by a child in the environment with the broken mother. Substances may be sought to get relief from stress or somatic reactions to interactions with the unhealthy mother or the chaotic home environment. Repeated functional use can progress to dependence and eventually to addiction. The goal of the substance abuse is often to numb somatic emotional sensations and to avoid thinking or obsessing about negative encounters or experiences. This behavior can have huge effects on the adult child's kids.

Self-Mutilation

Having an absent, abusive, or neglectful mother can cause the child to self-injure. Many who self-injure report that the function of this behavior is to:

- self-punish (due to feelings of guilt or shame)
- move out of a dissociative or numbed state (to feel something—to feel alive)
- see a physical manifestation of suppressed or buried emotions

Unfortunately, this is a cycle of behavior. Most of the time, it leads to deeper shame and guilt, which reinforces the original emotional pain. Also complicating this issue is that notwithstanding its gruesome symbolism, self-harm often functions as a coping mechanism that momentarily alleviates overwhelming suffering.

Running Away from Home

Avoidance is a common coping skill used by those people who have suffered familial trauma. Like substance abuse, running away is a form of avoidance or even denial. While running away may seem like an escape, it typically holds much more severe consequences, such as homelessness and exploitation. Illicit activities while being on the streets (e.g., dealing drugs, stealing, or prostituting oneself) can produce a harsh reality for those seeking safety and solace.

Runaways often expose themselves to numerous risks while having no means of supporting themselves. The behavior of avoidance can result in the adult parent abandoning his or her own kids when things get difficult. The negative reinforcement associated with absence can be rewarding for the wounded little kid who lies within the adult.

Eating Disorders

Like perfectionism and substance abuse, eating disorders involve an element of power and control. They can manifest as the result of enduring a childhood with an unhealthy mother. The patterns of unhealthy eating and body-image distortions are a manifestation of unmet needs and unexpressed emotions. Besides childhood familial issues, other confounding variables, such as social media and friends' influence, may play a significant role in developing an eating disorder. Commonly known eating disorders include anorexia nervosa, bulimia nervosa, and binge-eating disorder.

Many issues can manifest from momma trauma. All types of unhealthy mothers create unique challenges for the developing child. It is not uncommon for children to be affected by these types of unhealthy mothers throughout their lifespans if help and healing are not sought.

However, whatever maladaptive unhealthy behaviors result from having one of these types of unhealthy mother, the responsibility of healing falls on the adult child. Recognizing the impact of having an unhealthy mother is essential to deciding to heal. An unhealed adult child or mother figure will not necessarily become exactly like her mother figure. However, the trauma from having an unhealthy mother may negatively affect her understanding of mothering and her ability to mother in a healthy manner.

Reflection Questions

1. What positive coping skills did you develop growing up to survive living with an unhealthy mother? How have these served you in adulthood?
2. What negative coping skills did you develop growing up to survive living with an unhealthy mother? How have you dealt with these negative coping skills in adulthood?

CHAPTER 10
HEALING THE WOUNDED CHILD WITHIN

The book *I Am Me: A Girl, a Lady, and a Woman: Embracing All Aspects of the True Self* explores the process of healing the wounded inner self. Many talk about leaving the past in the past, but if we don't resolve trauma from the past, it tends to manifest in the present as we navigate the world in our personal and professional lives. For some people, healing involves accessing the wounded child who experienced the trauma of not having the mother who was needed. After that, a reparenting process can start. This reparenting process can be done on one's own using self-help manuals or can be resolved in a therapeutic setting with a counselor or psychologist. In addition to formal counseling, parenting classes and family sessions are also helpful in breaking generational patterns of dysfunction.

Some parents find that their healing process takes place naturally as they make a conscious decision to be a parent unlike the unhealthy parent that they had. These parents access their inner wounded child through playing with their own children. This may look like getting in the sand and making a sandcastle for one's child, playing dress-up, or riding on a roller coaster with their child.

Healing becomes difficult when the mother continues to be overly self-critical of the mistakes that she's making as she's navigating the healing process. It can be discouraging to find herself becoming like the critical mother that she had. It can be even harder if she recognizes that although she's trying, she resorts to the same type of unhealthy mothering that she received, especially when feeling overwhelmed,

It's important to have patience, grace, and forgiveness for self. Perfection is not the goal of the healing process. The goal is consistency and accountability, traits of the good imperfect mother. The good imperfect mother is the subject of the next chapter.

Reflection Questions

1. If you have attachment trauma that has resulted in an insecure attachment, what do you think that the healing process would look like for you?
2. What steps have you made in your healing journey?
3. What is difficult for you or confusing to you about the healing process?

CHAPTER 11
THE GOOD IMPERFECT MOTHER

There are many definitions of a good imperfect mother that came from the subjective disclosures of those who contributed to this book. Some mothers reading this book may recognize that they do not measure up to what has been defined as the good mother based on traditional roles and expectations. Such readers may feel pressured to live up to those roles; however, the healthy mother—even though imperfect—contributes to the child's development through how she nurtures and teaches her child. Depending on culture, mothering can look different. Cultural factors are important when assessing whether a mother is healthy or unhealthy.

Each of the mother's children may have different needs, and meeting those needs may be challenging when considering other important confounding variables. These may interfere with a woman's mothering abilities. Such variables include:

- the age of the mother
- the state of the mother's mental health
- single motherhood
- poverty
- lack of social resources
- the mother's understanding of motherhood
- the mother's relationship with her own mother
- the number of children that the mother has

Despite these variables, a good mother is consistent and accountable. She is as consistent as possible with providing for her children's basic needs. She can be counted on to follow through with what she says she'll do when it comes to meeting her kids' needs.

She is accountable. When she makes mistakes, she takes responsibility for them, which is how she teaches her kids to do the same thing. She teaches by her actions, displaying humility. For example, if she gets angry and takes the anger out on her kids, she apologizes and validates her kids' feelings. If she struggles with being warm, attentive, and responsive to her kids, when she becomes aware of this deficiency, she works to improve her mothering skills. She understands the impact of her mothering on the kids. She is:

- consistent
- accountable
- warm
- affectionate
- attentive

She understands that it is important for her kids to feel:

- *Loved.* This is demonstrated through her consistent actions.
- *Valued.* Children need to feel that they are an important priority.
- *Understood.* Children need to feel heard and to have their needs and feelings validated.
- *Supported.* Children need to feel that Mom will be there when they are faced with social challenges.

These behaviors can reinforce secure attachment. Dan Seigal identified four aspects of secure attachment—feeling:

- safe
- secure
- seen
- soothed

Kids need to feel *safe* with their mothers and protected. It is the protection and consistency of their needs being met that makes them feel *secure*. Children need to be *seen* for who they are and validated for who they are. They need to feel that they are an important part of their mom's life. They also need to be *soothed* or comforted when they get hurt (physically or emotionally).

Although these tasks and characteristics of the mother appear to be straightforward or even easy for some, what makes them challenging for some moms is that she is expected to mother in a manner that may seem foreign to her because she may not have a healthy frame of reference from which she can draw. She is expected to mother—even if she has not been mothered properly. Sometimes the broken mother needs to heal to mother her children in a healthy manner.

Reflection Questions

1. How would you describe the characteristics of a good mother?
2. Where did your ideas about the good mother come from? From your own mom? Relatives? The Internet? Movies? Television dramas or sitcoms? Friends?
3. Do you believe that a mother who has made mistakes unintentionally and has harmed her kids can be instrumental in her kids' healing even if they are adults?
4. Do you have trouble accepting the concept of the good imperfect mother or in seeing yourself as a good imperfect mother?

BIBLIOGRAPHY

Coles, R. L. (2009). *The best kept secret: Single black fathers*. Rowman & Littlefield Publishers.

Collins, P. H. (2000). *Black feminist thought: Knowledge, consciousness, and the politics of empowerment* (2nd ed.). Routledge.

Dorais, L. J. (2007). *The Vietnamese in Canada*. Canadian Historical Association.

Douglas, S. J., & Michaels, M. W. (2004). *The mommy myth: The idealization of motherhood and how it has undermined women*. Free Press.

Dube, S. R., Anda, R. F., Felitti, V. J., Edwards, V. J., & Croft, J. B. (2002). Adverse childhood experiences and personal alcohol abuse as an adult. *Addictive Behaviors, 27*(5), 713–725.

Falicov, C. J. (2005). Mexican families. In M. McGoldrick, J. Giordano, & N. Garcia-Preto (Eds.), *Ethnicity and family therapy* (3rd ed., pp. 229–241). Guilford Press.

Franklin, J. H., & Moss, A. A. (1988). *From slavery to freedom: A history of African Americans*. Knopf Doubleday Publishing Group.

Galanti, G. A. (2003). The Hispanic family and male–female relationships: An overview. *Journal of Transcultural Nursing, 14*(3), 180–185.

Gonzales, P. (2012). *Red medicine: Traditional indigenous rites of birthing and healing*. University of Arizona Press.

Hattery, A. (2001). *Women, work, and family: Balancing and weaving*. SAGE Publications.

Hays, S. (1996). *The cultural contradictions of motherhood*. Yale University Press.

Herman, J. L. (1992). *Trauma and recovery: The aftermath of violence—from domestic abuse to political terror*. Basic Books.

Kim, E., & Hong, S. (2007). First-generation Korean-American parents' perceptions of discipline. *Journal of Professional Nursing, 23*(1), 60–68.

Kimmel, M. S. (2013). *Manhood in America: A cultural history*. Oxford University Press.

Lamb, M. E. (Ed.). (2010). *The role of the father in child development* (5th ed.). John Wiley & Sons.

Lanius, R. A., Vermetten, E., & Pain, C. (2010). *The impact of early life trauma on health and disease: The hidden epidemic*. Cambridge University Press.

Lareau, A. (2003). *Unequal childhoods: Class, race, and family life*. University of California Press.

BIBLIOGRAPHY

Miller, T. (2007). *Making sense of motherhood: A narrative approach*. Cambridge University Press.

Pleck, J. H. (2010). Paternal involvement: Revised conceptualization and theoretical linkages with child outcomes. In M. E. Lamb (Ed.), *The role of the father in child development* (5th ed., pp. 58–93). John Wiley & Sons.

Rhee, S. H., Chang, J. M., & Rhee, J. (2003). Acculturation, communication patterns, and self-esteem among Asian and Caucasian American adolescents. *Adolescence, 38*(152), 749–768.

Springer, K. W., Sheridan, J., Kuo, D., & Carnes, M. (2007). Long-term physical and mental health consequences of childhood physical abuse: Results from a large population-based sample of men and women. *Child Abuse & Neglect, 31*(5), 517–530.